Copyright © 1989, 1996 by Empak Publishing Company

ISBN 0-922162-7-7 (Volume VII)
ISBN 0-922162-15-8 (Volume Set)

Library of Congress Cataloging-in-Publication Data

A Salute to Historic Black Firsts.
  p.   cm. – (An Empak "Black history" publication series ; vol. 7)
  Cover title.
  Includes bibliographical references.
  Summary: Presents biographical sketches of twenty-four black men and women who made notable contributions in the fields of government, education, law, journalism, religion, medicine, sports, and the arts.
  ISBN 0-922162-07-7
    1. Afro-Americans – Biography – Juvenile literature. 2. Afro-Americans – Miscellanea – Juvenile literature. 3. World records – Juvenile literature. [1. Afro-American – Biography. 2. United States – Biography.] I. Series: Empak "Black history" publication series : v. 7.
E185.96.S243 1996   95-48501
920'.009296073–dc20   CIP
[B]   AC

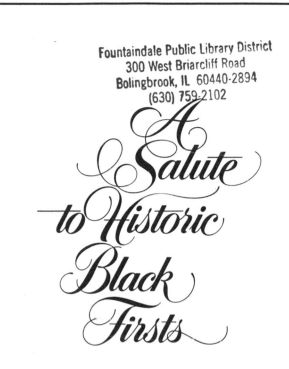

EMPAK PUBLISHING COMPANY

Published by Empak Publishing Company
212 East Ohio Street, Chicago, IL 60611.

Publisher & Editor: Richard L. Green
Assoc. Editors: Melody M. McDowell, Sylvia Shepherd
Researcher: Melody M. McDowell
Production: Dickinson & Associates, Inc.
Illustration: S. Gaston Dobson
Foreword: Empak Publishing Co.

To be *first* takes a special kind of person—someone willing to standout from the crowd and be counted. It also takes a person who is willing to bear the burden of sacrifice and responsibility that comes with such a significant distinction.

People who are *first* clear the path for all who come after them. And, when a Black person breaks a barrier and ventures into never-before-territory, the significance of his or her action is even more dynamic because of the effort which is required to overcome discrimination and dispel stereotype myths. Notwithstanding, the accomplishment of a *first* by a Black person holds out a shining ray of hope for all to see—a beacon to the path of self-realization and a meaningful life.

Each of the 24 individuals in this booklet overcame heavy odds on his or her way into history and our lives. Each represents a tremendous accomplishment, whether we examine the superlative intellectual achievement of Alain Locke or the steady and determined military rise of Gen. Benjamin Oliver Davis, Sr., each depicts a person of decision and action. Each had a vision, a goal, and a purpose.

As we strive to open doors of opportunity and plow new fields, homage should be extended to those who came before us, and recognition bestowed for the tremendous price they paid. By being *first*, they stood where all could see. Often viewed with the expectation of failure, they bore the weight of their race on their shoulders and they proved worthy.

It should be noted that the historic people mentioned in this booklet are only a very few of the many, many Black pioneers. To compile a truly comprehensive biography of all Black *firsts* would be an immense project that would run into numerous volumes. With this booklet, we have tried to present an array of "firsts" which represents many different disciplines and endeavors.

A Salute to Historic Black Firsts continues Empak's tradition of publishing affordable booklets that raise the consciousness and promotes the ethnic pride of Black America, while also providing a storehouse of knowledge of one's own history. This booklet continues the vision and purpose which the founders of Empak

Publishing Company nurtured when its Black history series was initially conceived.

In pursuit of our objective, we at Empak are proud to add this volume *(A Salute to Historic Black Firsts)* to our existing, highly acclaimed series. Each booklet is diverse and addresses a different theme and historic Black individuals, thereby demonstrating that the Black experience provides an almost endless array of positive achievements and contributions which begs conveyance to the masses of people.

Empak Publishing Company

CONTENTS

BIOGRAPHIES:

Dr. Ralph J. Bunche 8

Shirley Chisholm... 10

Gen. Benjamin 0. Davis, Sr................................. 12

James Derham 14

Paul Laurence Dunbar 16

Henry 0. Flipper... 18

Patricia Roberts Harris 20

Bishop James Healy 22

Jack Johnson... 24

Joshua Johnston 26

John Mercer Langston... 28

Alain Leroy Locke 30

Thurgood Marshall 32

Oscar Micheaux.. 34

Isaac Murphy.. 36

Jesse Owens.. 38

Jackie Robinson 40

John Sweat Rock.. 42

John B. Russwurm... 44

William S. Scarborough.. 46

William Grant Still.. 48

Denmark Vesey 50

Dr. Daniel Hale Williams.................................... 52

George Washington Williams 54

TEST YOURSELF 57

CROSSWORD PUZZLE 58

WORDSEARCH.. 59

QUIZ & GAME ANSWERS 60

Editor's Note: Due to this booklet's space limitations, some facets on the lives of the above noted Historic Black Firsts have been omitted.

DR. RALPH J. BUNCHE
1904 -1971

In 1950, Dr. Ralph Johnson Bunche achieved what no other diplomat had been able to accomplish; successfully end the first Arab-Israeli War. For this, he was awarded the Nobel Peace Prize, thus becoming the first Black to receive this prestigious honor. While Ralph came from humble roots, he rose to become a political scientist, an educator, a government official, and a great statesman.

Ralph Bunche was born in Detroit, Michigan, on August 7, 1904, the grandson of a slave. His father was a barber and his mother an amateur musician. Ralph and his sister were raised by their maternal grandmother, Lucy Johnson, in Los Angeles. Money was very scarce during Ralph Bunche's early schooling, so he had to work his way through Jefferson High School, and he graduated with top honors.

While attending the University of California at Los Angeles, Bunche distinguished himself in football, baseball, and basketball, and as a scholar who graduated, *summa cum laude*, in 1927. To supplement his athletic scholarship, he worked as a campus janitor. From UCLA, he entered Harvard University, with the help of friends and relatives, and earned his master's degree, in 1928, in government.

Also, in 1928, Bunche was appointed a professor of political science at Howard University. In 1930, at the age of 26, he married Ruth Harris, and they eventually had three children. In 1934, his educational quest returned him to Harvard, where he earned his doctorate.

In 1936, Bunche published a treatise, *A World View of Race*, which was so impressive that Gunnar Myrdal, the world renowned sociologist from Sweden, who had specialized in the area of race relations, hired Bunche as his chief research assistant. The combination of these two great minds produced the book, *An American Dilemma*, which is known as a classic study of the American Black. During World War II, Bunche was called upon to serve in very sensitive governmental positions.

As an expert on Africa, he helped to make the Allied invasion of North Africa a success. He became the first Black to hold a desk job at the U.S. State Department. And, he also helped lay the groundwork for the United Nations.

Ralph Bunche's diplomatic skill came to the attention of world leaders and, in 1946, UN Secretary General Trygve Lie appointed him to the trusteeship division of the United Nations, where he became intensely familiar with the dynamics of the explosive Arab-Israeli crisis. In 1947, he became a member of the UN Special Committee on Palestine, which advised partition of the country into Jewish and Arab states.

Tension between the two countries ignited the first Arab-Israeli War and touched off a series of events that led to the UN mediator being assassinated. Bunche was elevated to the position of chief mediator in 1946. After six months of intense negotiating, Bunche achieved an armistice. In 1950, he was rewarded the ultimate recognition for his skill; the Nobel Peace Prize, the first of his race to be so honored. His efforts also earned him awards from a host of organizations, including the NAACP Spingarn award, and the Medal of Freedom from President John F. Kennedy in 1963.

Bunche next negotiated peace-keeping initiatives in the Suez, the Congo and in Cyprus. In the Congo, he worked 19 hours a day, for weeks, as the head of a 20,000-man UN peace-keeping force. In 1962, at the age of 58, exhaustion from overwork made him consider retirement, but he stayed on at the urging of many people, including President Lyndon Johnson. And, he later became involved in the UN efforts to deploy nuclear energy for peaceful means.

In October of 1971, ill health finally forced Dr. Ralph Bunche to resign his post as Secretary General for Special Political Affairs, and he died in New York City, on December 9th. He was eulogized by UN Secretary-General U Thant as "the most effective and best-known international civil servant."

SHIRLEY A. CHISHOLM
1924 -

Shirley Anita Chisholm earned her place in history as the first Black woman elected to the United States Congress, and also as the first woman, White or Black, to make a serious bid for the presidency.

Shirley Chisholm was born on November 30, 1924, in Brooklyn, New York, one of four daughters of Charles and Ruby St. Hill, who both hailed from the West Indies. Her father was an unskilled laborer and her mother a seamstress and domestic, whose primary goal was to see to it that their children received a good education.

She attended a Brooklyn girls' high school and then entered Brooklyn College, where she earned a B.A. *cum laude* in 1946, majoring in sociology. She subsequently attended Columbia University, where she earned an M.A. degree in elementary education, and she became an authority on early education and child welfare. She also developed an interest in Black history and the issue of civil rights. Harriet Tubman, the fearless Black conductor on the Underground Railroad, and Susan B. Anthony, a suffragette, were among her heroines.

Shirley Chisholm became increasingly involved in the community and, anxious to be in a position where she could dramatically forge change, she entered politics. Directly accountable to the people rather than to so-called party bosses, she campaigned without the blessing of the Democratic Party machine, and she was elected to the New York State Assembly in 1964, the first Black woman ever elected to the position. During her four years in the statehouse, nine of her own bills were passed by the assembly and four were signed into law.

In 1968, Shirley Chisholm brought her political aspirations into the national arena, when she was drafted to run as a Democratic candidate for Congress. Yielding to the wishes of the people, Mrs. Chisholm warded off stiff primary and Republican challenges. On November 5, 1968, she was elected to the 91st Congress from Brooklyn, making her the first Black woman to serve in this legislative body.

Following her 1970 re-election, Chisholm wanted to carry her crusade, for the rights of the underserved, to even greater levels. On January 25, 1972, Chisholm uttered these history making words, "I hereby declare myself a candidate for President of the United States of America." While she didn't win the nomination, she made an impressive showing.

Shirley Chisholm's life is chronicled in her autobiography, *Unbought and Unbossed.* In 1973, she reflected on her presidential bid in her book, *The Good Fight.* After a successful 14-year Congressional career, she returned to her first love, education, in 1983, and became a teacher at Mt. Holyoke College in Massachusetts. In *The Good Fight,* Shirley Chisholm explained why she ran for the presidency: "I ran for the presidency in order to crack a little more of the ice which in recent years has congealed to nearly immobilize our political system and demoralize people. I ran for the presidency, despite hopeless odds, to demonstrate sheer will and refusal to accept the status quo."

She also wrote, "My goal was to shake things up a little. I think I made a dent or two; time will tell. At any rate, I feel the Chisholm candidacy accomplished one thing. The next time a woman of whatever color, or dark-skinned person of whatever sex aspires to be President, the way should be a little smoother because I helped pave it. Perhaps some Black or Spanish-speaking child already dreams of running for the presidency some day, because a Black woman has dared to. That child's dream would be more than enough for me to have accomplished, would it not?"

GEN. BENJAMIN O. DAVIS, SR.
1877 - 1970

The first Black American to become a general in the United States Army was Benjamin Oliver Davis, Sr. In a military career that spanned 50 years, Davis saw action in the Spanish-American War, World War I, and World War II.

Benjamin Davis was born in Washington, D.C., on June 1, 1877, the grandson of a slave who had bought his own freedom in 1800. His father, Louis P. H. Davis, was a messenger in the Department of Interior in Washington. The primary task for overseeing the boy's upbringing fell on his mother, Henrietta. Davis was raised in Washington, D.C., where he attended public schools. It was while attending Howard University that he visited the Army base at nearby Fort Myer, Virginia, and was drawn to military life.

In 1898, Davis enlisted as a temporary first lieutenant in the 8th United States Infantry at the height of the Spanish-American War. One year later, he was mustered out. However, in June of 1899, his overwhelming desire to serve in the military motivated him to re-enlist as a private in the 9th Cavalry of the regular army. On February 2, 1900, he earned a second lieutenant's commission. Meanwhile, he met and married Elnora Dickerson in 1902. Out of this union, three children were born.

Because of racial discrimination, Davis often found himself passed over when promotions were granted. Undaunted, he served admirably in the Philippines and at Fort Washakie, Wyoming. His efforts were finally rewarded when he was promoted to first lieutenant in 1905. For ten years, Davis remained in this rank. In 1915, the World War I crisis enabled him to earn two rapid, but temporary, promotions; in 1917, he was made a major; in 1918, a lieutenant colonel. However, he was returned to his former rank of captain after the war. This setback notwithstanding, Davis persevered and, in 1920, he was promoted, permanently, to the rank of lieutenant colonel.

Davis added another dimension to his military portfolio when he became a professor of military tactics at Wilberforce University in Ohio, and later at Tuskeegee Institute in Alabama. He also was appointed as a military attache to Monrovia, Liberia, and became an instructor of the 372nd Infantry of the National Guard in Cleveland, Ohio.

In 1940, after a decade of being denied promotions, Davis was temporarily elevated to the rank of Brigadier General as World War II spread. Davis retired from military service on July 31, 1941. He was immediately recalled to active duty and given the permanent rank of Brigadier General. It was during this period that he played a major troubleshooting role in implementing the policy of military racial integration. From 1945 until his retirement in 1948, Davis served in strategic administrative roles to the Inspector-General of the Army and the Secretary of the Army.

During his remaining years, Davis lived in Washington, D.C., and watched with pride his son, Benjamin Oliver Davis, Jr., ascend the military ladder. On October 27, 1954, Benjamin 0. Davis, Jr., became the first Black Brigadier General in the history of the U.S. Air Force and, in 1965, he rose to the rank of Lieutenant General—achievements that paralleled his father's illustrious accomplishments.

Benjamin 0. Davis, Sr. basked in his memories of a distinguished career that earned him a host of honors, including the Bronze Star, the French Croix de Guerre with Palm and the Distinguished Service Medal. However, on November 26, 1970, he passed away at the Great Lakes Naval Hospital in Illinois. Davis' life had been one of steady determination. He persevered and advanced under circumstances and conditions where others would have failed.

DR. JAMES DERHAM
1762 - 1805 (?)

In the days when many physicians had practical rather than formal training, James Derham rose from the depths of slavery to become the first prominent Black medical practitioner in the United States. At the height of his career, he was one of the nations foremost specialists in throat disorders.

Derham was born a slave on May 1, 1762, in Philadelphia. While there are no early records of his first owner, his subsequent masters were all doctors, who taught him the skills to care for the sick. His first known master was Dr. John Kearsley, Jr., a Philadelphia doctor, who specialized in sore throat ailments.

Under Kearsley's careful guidance, young James learned how to mix medical formulas and treat patients. After Kearsley's anti-war activities led to his imprisonment and death, Derham was purchased by a surgeon of the 16th British Regiment, Dr. George West. Under West, Derham increased his medical knowledge. By the time he was sold to the Scottish physician, Dr. Robert Dove, who lived in New Orleans, Derham had become a highly skilled doctor.

Dr. Dove was so impressed by Derham's medical skills that he not only allowed him to purchase his own freedom for 500 pesos on April 2, 1783, but Dove also helped him establish a medical practice. Derham married and opened up his practice to all races. His annual income of $3,000 was considered very substantial at that time.

Accompanied by his wife, a journey to Philadelphia to be baptized proved to be fortunate for Derham's career because he met Dr. Benjamin Rush, at the time America's foremost physician. Rush observed Derham in action and admired his medical proficiency as well as his fluency in Spanish and French. On November 14, 1788, Rush wrote a letter to the Pennsylvania Abolitionist Society extolling Derham's skills. The letter stated, in part, "I have conversed with him on most of the acute and epidemic diseases ... and was pleased to find him perfectly acquainted with the modern simple mode of practice in those diseases. I expected to have suggested some new medicines to him, but he suggested many more to me."

The two doctors developed a mutual admiration that caused Rush to take an intense interest in James Derham's career. When Derham returned to New Orleans, he authored the treatise, "An Account of the Putrid Sore Throat at New Orleans." Dr. Rush presented the paper before the College of Physicians of Philadelphia and that paper firmly established Derham as a national medical authority on the relationship of disease to climate.

New Orleans was struck by a yellow fever epidemic in 1796, and Derham was pressed into service. Those patients who sought his services were given his personally developed concoction of "garden sorrel and sugar" that was so successful he lost fewer patients than other doctors.

Despite his medical ability, in 1801, Derham was restricted by the New Orleans City Council from practicing because he and others like him was unlicensed and non-degreed. Derham's exceptional skills, however, forced the Council to rescind this dictate and allowed him to continue to treat throat maladies.

Dr. Derham continued to make significant medical contributions until his death, sometime between 1802 and 1805. His medical compatriot, Dr. Benjamin Rush, remained a devout supporter of his, singing Derham's praises to the medical community nationwide until Rush himself died in 1813.

PAUL LAURENCE DUNBAR
1872 - 1906

Poetry, novels, short stories, magazine articles and song lyrics; all these literary forms were mastered by Paul Laurence Dunbar. Because he was the first Black person recognized nationally as a creative writer, he was known as the "poet laureate of his people."

Paul Laurence Dunbar was born in Dayton, Ohio, in 1872, the son of Joshua and Matilda Dunbar, both former slaves. As a child, he displayed a propensity for writing; and while attending Central High in Dayton, he was elected president of the literary society, editor of the school paper, and creator of the class song sung at his graduation in 1891. He was the only Black in his high school class.

Dunbar wanted to attend college, but funds were short, so he had to take a job as an elevator operator, making $4.00 a week. While operating the elevator, he spent idle time writing verses. He eventually developed a style of writing in Black dialect as well as in simple verse. Dunbar refined his poetry and approached a publisher of a local newspaper who was so impressed that he printed the poems. In 1891, *The Rochester Herald* became the first newspaper to print a Dunbar poem.

By 1892, when he was 20, Dunbar had become so dedicated that he devoted full-time to his writing. In December, 1892, a publisher accepted his first collection of poems entitled, *Oak and Ivy.* With the publication of this collection, he gained notoriety and a legion of fans, including the famed critic William Dean Howells. It was largely due to Howells' endorsement of his work that Dunbar gained a greater following and became a fixture on the lecture circuit.

Dunbar was asked to speak at a variety of assemblies, including the West End Club of Toledo, Ohio. On that occasion, the participants prior to Dunbar making his presentation, denounced Blacks as intellectually inferior. Dunbar gave his recitation and chose to read a poem that expressed race pride. His reading was a poetic answer to the racial insults.

Oak and Ivy was enthusiastically received and the public asked for more. He quickly published his second volume, *Majors and Minors,* which won rave reviews in *Harper's* magazine in 1894. Dunbar's work attracted publishers and, in 1896 when he was only 24, a major publishing house produced his third collection, *Lyrics of Lowly Life.* The volume was immensely popular and firmly established Dunbar as a successful writer.

Sparked by the reception of his works, Dunbar produced additional volumes of poetry and, branching out, tried his hand, successfully, at four novels and articles for such highly-regarded publications as the *Saturday Evening Post.* His appearances on the lecture circuit also increased.

Dunbar married Alice Ruth Moore, a schoolteacher, in 1898, but the pace of success took its toll on his physical condition and his marriage. In the span of a decade, he wrote three short story collections and a novel entitled, *The Uncalled.* Churning out such a volume of work in such a brief period of time had a harmful effect on him. He contracted tuberculosis and this condition was aggravated by his drinking. His marriage failed and, on February 9, 1906, he died of pneumonia.

Because Paul Laurence Dunbar only lived to be 34, one can only imagine what heights he could have reached had he lived longer. Nevertheless, in penning his obituary, *The Boston Evening Transcript* attempted to capture his importance by noting, "He has given value and permanence to the folklore of the race in this country." Life had ended too soon for the man that Frederick Douglass had once called "the most promising young colored man in America."

HENRY OSSIAN FLIPPER
1856 - 1940

At the 1877 graduation exercises at West Point, only one graduate received cheers, Henry Ossian Flipper, former slave and the first Black to graduate from the United States Military Academy. He would go on to further distinguish himself as an engineer and a valued advisor to the U.S. government.

Flipper was born a slave in Thomasville, Georgia, in 1856, the son of Festus and Isabella Flipper. His father, a skilled worker, bought his wife and children's freedom and guided their educational path so effectively that all of his five children became successful professionals.

Following the signing of the *Emancipation Proclamation* in 1863, and the Civil War in 1865, the Flipper family was able to move to Atlanta, where Henry enrolled in the American Missionary School and later, Atlanta University, the institution from which he received his appointment to West Point. Flipper was at first shunned by the White cadets at West Point, and in his 1878 memoirs, *The Colored Cadet at West Point,* he graphically described how he was treated. Nevertheless, he graduated 50th out of a class of 76, in 1877. This event was so significant that the media converged upon West Point to see history in the making.

Despite having graduated from West Point with other White cadets, the Army's racial policy barred Blacks from serving in all-White units. Therefore, upon receiving his commission as second lieutenant, he was assigned, in January of 1878, to the all-Black 10th Cavalry Regiment, a unit the Indians dubbed the "Buffalo Soldiers."

In 1881, after serving honorably with this unit, he was assigned to Fort Davis, in Texas. There, he occasionally took horseback rides with one of the few White women in the area, a habit that enraged his white superiors. After this, he was arrested and charged with embezzlement of nearly $4,000 of commissary funds and conduct "unbecoming an officer and gentleman." He was unable to produce the money and was found guilty of the "conduct" charge. On June 30, 1882, he was dismissed from the army. For the remainder of his life, Flipper attempted to clear his name. He appealed for a review of his case, insisting that the Army's record of discrimination was the sole basis for the manufacturing of the charges. He turned to Booker T. Washington for assistance, but his efforts were in vain as the request for a review was denied.

Failing in his campaign, Flipper went on to distinguish himself as an engineer, miner and surveyor. His knowledge of Mexico and its impact on the American economy, plus his fluency in Spanish, made him a valuable employee and earned him high-level governmental appointments. Between 1892 and 1903, he was a special agent of the Department of Justice in the Court of Private Land Claims and later became an assistant to the Secretary of the Interior.

Flipper worked for an oil company in Venezuela, from 1923 to 1930, and he witnessed the beginning of a new energy age. He then moved to Atlanta to live with his brother, Joseph. There, he died in 1940 of a heart attack.

In death, Henry O. Flipper achieved the recognition he so desperately sought when he was alive. In 1976, the Army cleared him of all charges and, on May 3, 1977, West Point paid tribute to him by unveiling a bust in his honor. This ceremony was conducted in the presence of his relatives, two West Point regiments, and other Black cadets who followed Flipper. At the commemoration, Lt. General Sidney B. Berry, superintendent, described Flipper as "one of the most honored citizens of the nation, a credit to all of its people and its rich diversity."

PATRICIA ROBERTS HARRIS
1924 -1985

Patricia Roberts Harris represents two firsts: She was the first Black woman to serve in a president's cabinet and the first Black to serve as Secretary in two cabinet posts. In 1977, President Jimmy Carter appointed her to his cabinet as Secretary of Housing and Urban Development. In 1979, she was appointed Secretary of Health and Human Services.

Patricia Harris' rise to historic prominence was preceded by an equally impressive background. She was born on May 31, 1924, in Mattoon, IL. She graduated, *summa cum laude*, with a B.A. degree from Howard University in 1945. While at Howard, she was elected Phi Beta Kappa. She did postgraduate work at the University of Chicago and the American University in 1949. Until 1953, she worked as Assistant Director of the American Council on Human Rights in keeping with her interest in, and sensitivity to, this subject.

While at Howard, she met William Beasley Harris, a member of the Howard law faculty. They were married in 1955. She then earned a law degree with honors from George Washington University in 1960. Graduating number one out of a class of 94, she was admitted to practice before the U.S. Supreme Court. Attorney Harris worked briefly for the U.S. Department of Justice before returning, in 1961, to Howard University as an associate dean of students and law lecturer at Howard's law school. In 1963, she was elevated to a full professorship and, in 1969, she was named Dean of Howard University's School of Law.

Even while she was a student at Howard University, she was interested in politics. As her adult life took shape, she parlayed her interest in political activism into a career path that would bring her to the attention of political leaders.

Her first position with the U.S. government was as an attorney in the appeals and research section of the criminal division of the Department of Justice in 1960. There she met and struck up a friendship with Robert Kennedy, the new attorney general. In 1963, President John F. Kennedy appointed her co-chairman of the National Women's Committee for Civil Rights.

In 1964, Patricia Harris was elected a delegate to the Democratic National Convention from the District of Columbia. She worked in Lyndon Johnson's presidential campaign and seconded his nomination at the 1964 Democratic Convention. Soon after his victory, President Johnson appointed her Ambassador to Luxembourg from 1965 to 1967. Following her service as Dean of Howard's School of Law, from 1969 to 1972, she joined one of Washington, D.C.'s most prestigious law firms.

She continued making an impact on the Democratic Party when, in 1972, she was appointed chairman of the credentials committee and a member-at-large of the Democratic National Committee in 1973. A testimony to her effectiveness her and commitment to excellence came when President Jimmy Carter appointed her to two cabinet level posts during his administration.

At the Senate confirmation committee to approve her appointment, one senator tried to suggest that Patricia Harris' position might make her ill-qualified to represent the underclass. To this, she shot back, "I am one of them. You do not seem to understand who I am. I am a Black woman, the daughter of a dining-car worker. I am a Black woman who could not buy a house eight years ago in parts of the District of Columbia."

In 1982, Patricia Harris was appointed a full-time professor at the George Washington National Law Center, a position she served in until her death on March 23, 1985. She had always been aware of her roots and was well-known for her feistiness.

■ BISHOP JAMES AUGUSTINE HEALY ■
1830 -1900

A plantation slave with an Irish name, James Augustine Healy became the first Black Catholic priest and bishop in the United States.

James Healy was born on a Jones County, Georgia, plantation on April 6, 1830. He was the product of mixed parentage. James' father was a wealthy Irishman, Michael Morris Healy, and his mother was Healy's mulatto slave, Mary Eliza Smith. Even though his father was White, James and his nine younger brothers and sisters were still regarded as slaves because of their mother's status.

James' father was a rebel, defying Georgia laws by marrying a slave. He left his $40,000 estate to his children. James was to make the best of his opportunities, eventually becoming the Roman Catholic bishop of Portland, Maine, the spiritual leader of 80,000 Catholics, only 300 of whom were Black.

Michael Healy wanted his children to be as free as he was, so he took them to Flushing, Long Island, in 1837, and enrolled James and his brothers in a Quaker school. Seven years later, James was transferred to the Jesuit College of Holy Cross in Worcester, Massachusetts, where he earned both a bachelor's degree in 1849 and a master's in 1851.

After the death of his parents in 1850, he followed the urgings of his father's influential friends and decided to become a priest. With his sights on this goal, he studied at the Grand Seminary in Montreal and was ordained at the Sulpician Seminary in Paris a Catholic priest in the famed Cathedral of Notre Dame in Paris, in June, 1854. Following his ordination, he returned to America as the first Black priest in the United

States. Bishop John Fitzpatrick brought Healy into the Boston diocese to serve as his secretary and chancellor.

At the height of the Civil War, Healy was appointed pastor of the Cathedral of the Holy Cross. Following the War, in 1866, he was appointed pastor of St. James, the largest church in Boston, which had a primarily Irish congregation.

Overtures of racism were dispelled by Healy's sensitivity during Boston's typhoid, tuberculosis and influenza epidemic. He visited the sick, offering sacraments and last rites. The congregation was also moved by his eloquent messages and sincerity. He became a champion of social issues as he created programs to care for destitute, homeless and incorrigible children; and he defended immigrants and those confined in public institutions. Because he advocated these initiatives with such zeal, he became known as "The Children's Bishop." His compassion for the needy compelled him to pay their overdue taxes, to settle their hospital bills, and to purchase food and clothes for them.

By 1875, Healy's reputation for effectiveness and eloquence had gained international attention and he was appointed, by Pope Pius IX, as bishop of the states of Maine and New Hampshire. This appointment automatically earned Healy a berth in the history books because he could now claim to be the first Black priest and the first Black bishop.

Despite this challenge, Bishop Healy was highly-regarded within the Catholic community. He enjoyed the friendship of both Pope Pius IX and Pope Leo XII, the latter appointing him an assistant to the papal throne. He was also revered by the hundreds of White priests who loyally served under him.

Bishop Healy died of a heart attack in Portland, Maine, on August 5, 1900. He was buried at a Catholic cemetery near Portland. As a memorial to him, one of the buildings at Holy Cross is named in his honor, as are other institutions in Maine and in other states where he served. Also, the 68 mission stations, 18 parochial schools, and 50 church buildings erected, while he was bishop, serve as a memorial to him.

JACK JOHNSON
1878 - 1946

Jack Johnson was the first Black heavyweight boxing champion of the world. While criticized by Whites for his lifestyle outside the ring, he is still regarded by some experts as the best heavyweight of all time.

Jack Johnson was born in Galveston, Texas, on March 31, 1878, the son of a school janitor. He was so small as a child that he earned the nickname, "Li'l Arthur." He quit school, after the fifth grade, and worked at odd jobs until he became big enough to work on the docks.

Johnson began boxing as a means of survival. As a dockhand in his native Galveston, he worked alongside those who provoked fights. Once, while in a brawl with another worker, his raw boxing skills were noticed and he was offered $25 to fight four rounds. Realizing that this was a better way to make a living, for someone nearly 6 foot 4 and 195 pounds, he accepted the challenge. Eventually, in bouts, he boxed his way across the United States. By 1906, he had won a phenomenal 97 out of 100 fights.

With this enviable record, Johnson was set to challenge the current heavyweight champion, Tommy Burns, of Australia. Because Johnson desperately wanted the fight, he agreed to outrageous terms that were so tilted in Burns' favor that Johnson had to dominate the fight. And dominate he did, beating Burns so decisively that the fight had to be stopped in the 14th round in Sydney, Australia, on December 26, 1908.

After this victory, Johnson returned to the United States as the undisputed heavyweight champion of the world. He continued to silence any doubters by easily defeating a string of challengers. Instead of welcoming the new champion, Whites resented his color and began to look for a "White hope." This search resulted in the successful persuasion of former heavyweight champion Jim Jeffries to leave retirement and to challenge Johnson in 1910. Because of what was at stake, the bout was known as the "Battle of the Century" and attracted a wide range of spectators. Jeffries fought bravely until the 14th round, but in the 15th, Johnson landed a left hook to the former champ that sent him reeling to the mat. This gave Johnson the undisputed crown.

Much of the resentment toward Johnson grew because of his high living and his relations with women. He often frequented nightspots with a White woman on his arm; he invested foolishly; and his unwillingness to accept insults with "dignity" resulted in arrests and other brushes with the law. Eventually, a legal charge caused by a failed romance forced him to flee the United States in 1913.

In his autobiography, *Jack Johnson in the Ring and Out*, he revealed that he was given the opportunity to return to America, if he would throw a championship fight to Jess Willard of Pottawatomie, Kansas. In Havana, Cuba, in 1915, the two went one-on-one in the ring for a phenomenal 25 rounds. Totally exhausted, Johnson was decked by a blow to the stomach in the 26th round, and Willard was declared the champion.

Following the match, Johnson lived in exile in Spain and Mexico before returning to America, in 1920, to serve 11 months in prison. Following his release, he earned his living by fighting in a series of exhibitions, where he proved that he still had the winning touch. However, he was virtually penniless.

Jack Johnson, who confessed a weakness for fast driving, died on June 11, 1946, in an automobile accident near Raleigh, North Carolina. In his life, he fought 113 recorded bouts in the ring, and in the difficult arena of trail blazing. He fought his last fight in 1945, at the age of 67. Jack Johnson was elected to boxing's Hall of Fame in 1954.

JOSHUA JOHNSTON
1765 - 1830

The first American Black to achieve status and recognition as a renowned portrait painter was Joshua Johnston.

During the latter part of the eighteenth century, Joshua Johnston was without doubt the premiere portrait artist for many aristocratic families. Even today, modern critics marvel at his skill in detail and lighting, which were mastered without any apparent formal training. He remains perhaps the most celebrated of the Afro-American artisan painters.

Joshua Johnston was born a slave and lived in the vicinity of Baltimore. He was owned by three well-regarded masters, two of whom were military leaders and one was a prosperous entrepreneur. These "masters" detected Johnston's natural artistic talents and his remarkable ability to "do likenesses."

Unlike some owners who discouraged their slaves from acquiring a skill or an education, Johnston's masters encouraged him to not only cultivate his talent, but also to earn a living at portrait painting. In fact, he was so self-assured of his ability that on December 19, 1798, he placed an ad in the *Baltimore Intelligencer* offering his services.

Johnston developed a style similar to that of another portrait artist of the day, Charles Wilson Peale, leading some experts to believe he might have studied under Peale. Johnston's subjects adopted a similar expression and were painted in oil, with a solid black background to accentuate their characteristics. He painted on canvasses that ranged in size from 18 by 24 inches to 50 by 70 inches. By minimizing background distractions, the full effect of the subject was clearly emphasized.

None of Johnston's paintings are signed, but they have similarities; Sheraton chairs and suites, white dresses, detailed lace and hair, cords and tassels. His subjects all stare directly at the viewer, their noses clearly outlined, but their hands seemingly boneless.

As testimony to their confidence in him, one of his masters, Col. John Moale, commissioned him to paint a portrait of his wife and their granddaughter in about 1800. By this time, historians believe Johnston was a free man and was referred to in Baltimore as a "Free Householder of Colour."

Johnston's portraits won praise from the Moale family and, apparently through word-of-mouth advertising, he contracted to paint portraits of many aristocratic families of the day; including Mr. Andrew Bedford Bankston (1804), Mrs. Thomas Kell and Daughter (1789-1790), the Kennedy Long Family (c. 1805), Benett Sollers (c.1810) and a host of others. His reputation grew and he became the leading portrait artist for many wealthy families in Maryland, Virginia and the east coast.

Since Johnston's death, his extraordinary talent has gained nationwide and worldwide admiration. A century after his death, his name was brought to the attention of the public by J. Hall Pleasants, who wrote of Johnston's early artistry.

Joshua Johnston's artistic legacy includes only 25 portraits definitely attributed to him, and another 25 that are possibly his work. Where once his paintings were the coveted possessions of individual families, his works now hang on public display at such prestigious museums as the National Gallery of Art, the Howard University Gallery of Art, the Baltimore Museum of Art, and the Fisk University Gallery of Art.

JOHN MERCER LANGSTON
1829-1897

John Mercer Langston earned his place in history as the first Black elected to public office in the United States, when he was elected an Ohio township clerk in 1855. He went on to become an elected U.S. Congressman, educator, lawyer, diplomat, and freedom fighter for Black causes.

John Langston was born in Louisa County, Virginia, the son of Capt. Ralph Quarles, a white plantation owner; and Lucy Langston, a slave of Black and Indian descent. When he was only five-years-old, both of his parents died; and the responsibility for caring for and educating him was placed on Col. William D. Gooch, an intimate friend of Langston's father.

John attended public school in Chillicothe, Ohio, where he came under the influence of George B. Vashon, the first Black graduate of Oberlin Ohio College, who encouraged him to attend Oberlin. There Langston received his B.A. and M.A. degrees in 1849 and 1852. While there, he also studied theology. As late as 1852, he favored emigration by Blacks from the U.S., but he later believed in the ultimate success of an integrated society.

His ambition to be a lawyer was temporarily prevented by law schools, which would not accept Blacks. Therefore, he learned the legal profession from Judge Philemon Bliss of Elyria, Ohio, who discovered a quirk in the law that qualified Langston to be "classified" a white man. Accordingly, he passed the bar exam and was admitted to the Ohio Bar in September, 1854. A month later he married Caroline M. Wall, a student at Oberlin College, with whom he had a daughter and three sons.

Langston, in 1864, was elected president of the National Equal Rights League, and he promoted the importance of the Black vote. From 1868 to 1869, he was inspector general of the

Freedmen's Bureau and was especially active in supporting Black educational opportunities.

His Black suffrage activities put him in direct conflict with Booker T. Washington and the NAACP, both of whom Langston dismissed as being out-of-step with the Black movement. He also made history when he was appointed the first dean of Howard University's Law School, which he had helped organize in 1869. After leaving Howard in 1876, Langston favored Republican Party politics; and this brought him to the attention of President Rutherford B. Hayes, whose candidacy Langston supported. In 1877, President Hayes made him the minister-resident and consul-general to Haiti, and charge d'affaires to the Dominican Republic. He held these posts until 1885 and proved an able representative of the U.S.

Upon returning to the United States, he served as president of Virginia Normal and Collegiate Institute from 1885 to 1888. Under his leadership, the institute grew and improved. With a well-earned reputation among Blacks and Whites, Langston chose Virginia as the state from which to make a serious political bid, and he announced his candidacy for the U.S. House of Representatives. Langston finally was seated by a vote of the U.S. House of Representatives and 51st Congress on September 23, 1890.

While in the House, he proposed a bill calling for an industrial university for Black youths. He criticized the harassment of Black voters in the South and, although he only served for six months, his place in history was secured. Langston failed in his bid to be reelected to the 52nd Congress and refused to accept a draft to run for the 53rd Congress, preferring instead to spend the remainder of his life lecturing on education, politics and economics.

Before his death, from a stroke in 1897, John Mercer Langston published some of his best speeches in *Freedom and Citizenship*. He also recorded the events of his diverse life in an autobiography, *From the Virginia Plantation to the National Capital*.

ALAIN LeROY LOCKE
1885 - 1954

The awarding of a Rhodes Scholarship carries with it the reputation of superior intellect and potential achievement. The first Black to become a Rhodes Scholar was Alain LeRoy Locke, and he would have to fulfill his early promise of greatness. The fact that Alain Locke rose to such intellectual heights was no surprise because he came from a background of educators.

Alain Locke was born in Philadelphia on September 13, 1885, the only child of Pliny Ishmael Locke and Mary Hawkins Locke. His father was a schoolteacher and a graduate of Howard University Law School.

When Alain Locke was a youngster, rheumatic fever left him with a permanently damaged heart. He found himself restricted primarily to intellectual and artistic pursuits. From 1898 to 1902, he attended Central High School of Philadelphia. He then earned a bachelor's degree at the Philadelphia School of Pedagogy, a teacher's college, where he graduated first in his class. After entering Harvard College, he completed a four-year course in three years. In 1907, he also won the prestigious Bowdoin Prize for an essay in English, was elected to Phi Beta Kappa, and received a B.A. degree, *magna cum laude*.

The act that gave him his special niche in the world's history books was his performance in a rigorous examination in Greek, Latin and mathematics for the Rhodes Scholarship. His selection in 1907, made him the first Black to become a Rhodes Scholar at Oxford University. Despite his intellectual accomplishments, he was not immune to racism. His admission request to five Oxford colleges was denied.

Finally, Locke was admitted to Hertford College and later to the University of Berlin from 1910 to 1911. While still a graduate student, he began writing about Black art and racism. His first book on race relations was to be published in

1918. His European experiences also gave him a global view of racism and an interest in African colonialism.

In 1912, he returned to the United States and was appointed to the faculty of the Teachers College at Howard University and later chairman of the philosophy department. He worked at Howard, intermittently, for 40 years. Locke continued to expand his educational horizons when he earned a doctorate from Harvard in 1918. In 1925, he made a profound impact with his book on Black cultural achievements called, *The New Negro.* This book brought him national attention. It contained essays interpreting the spirit of the famous Harlem Renaissance for the reading public.

Alain Locke fostered the Renaissance by discovering and helping young Black writers. He also had another motivation; he attacked racism by pointing out Black achievements to the White society. Because of this book, Locke became the main spokesman of what he called, "The New Negro Movement."

Locke also championed other art forms and pioneered the concept of Black theater as it is known today. His African arts collection became world renowned. And, he authored, along with T. Montgomery Gregory, an anthology of Black drama entitled, *Plays of Negro Life,* in 1927. By the end of World War II, Locke was one of the world's foremost scholars.

Locke was elected the first Black president of the American Association for Adult Education in 1945, a predominantly White, national education association. When Howard University began an African Studies Program in 1954, such a program had been suggested 30 years before by Locke. When Howard obtained a Phi Beta Kappa chapter in 1953, it was the result of 15 years of effort by Locke.

Alain Locke was sought after as a lecturer and received many other honors. However, his disease-damaged heart caused him to suffer a fatal heart attack on June 9, 1954. At the time of his death, he was collaborating with his associate, Margaret Just Butcher, on the book, *The Negro in American Culture.* She would later finish the book.

THURGOOD MARSHALL
1908 - 1993

When Thurgood Marshall was appointed and confirmed as a Supreme Court Justice, another page in history was recorded. He was the first Black to be elevated to this position. Reaching a position on the highest court in the nation culminated an illustrious legal career that had seen him successfully argue landmark cases that altered the racial fabric of America.

Thurgood was born on July 2, 1908, in Baltimore, the son of Norma, a schoolteacher, and William Canfield Marshall. He attended public schools in Baltimore and earned his bachelor's degree, *cum laude*, from Lincoln University in 1930. At first, he planned to study dentistry, but he switched his sights to law because of his father's influence. His father's insistence on logic and proof, pointed Marshall into a legal career.

Thurgood Marshall enrolled at Howard University in the pre-law program, after being denied admission to the University of Maryland Law School because of his race. This incident would later haunt the university. While at Howard, Marshall's civil rights thinking was shaped by a noted lawyer, Charles Houston, and a group of legal scholars concerned with the civil rights litigation.

In 1933, Marshall graduated from law school, *magna cum laude*, and subsequently passed the Maryland bar exam and began practicing law in his hometown of Baltimore. In 1929, he married Vivien G. Burney. Marshall's clients were poor and often unable to pay his fee. He became known as "the little man's lawyer," believing that the Constitution "was designed for the least as well as the greatest Americans."

Marshall's legal ability was immediately tested, when he became counsel for the Baltimore branch of the *NAACP*. In 1938, he became special counsel for the NAACP. He argued the case of *Sweatt v. Painter,* resulting in the ordering of the University of Texas Law School to admit Blacks. Because of

Marshall's own experience, he successfully fought the case with a particular zeal.

While serving as the NAACP's legal counsel, he added another dimension to his civil rights agenda when he co-founded the NAACP Legal Defense and Education Fund. There, he, and a group of lawyers, won 32 of the 35 cases they brought before the Supreme Court. By this time, Marshall had earned the well-deserved nickname, "Mr. Civil Rights."

In the 1950s, Marshall was dispatched to Korea to investigate charges that the Army was discriminating against Blacks. Until 1964, Marshall continued to argue cases that had legal reverberations nationwide. *Smith v. Allwright* (1944) established voting rights for Blacks. *Morgan v. Virginia* (1946) outlawed the state's segregation of interstate buses. *Shelley v. Kramer* (1948) barred restrictive covenants in housing. But his most celebrated case was *Brown v. the Board of Education of Topeka, Kansas* (1954), which removed the legal basis for segregation in public schools.

Marshall began his journey up the federal judicial ladder on September 23, 1961, when President John F. Kennedy nominated him as a judge of the Second Court of Appeals. Three years later, President Lyndon Johnson appointed him Solicitor General, the first Black to ever hold this post. This position set the stage for his nomination as associate Justice to the U.S. Supreme Court, in 1967, by President Johnson. After Senate confirmation, he joined this revered body as part of the liberal group of justices. Marshall worked on behalf of the economically, politically and legally deprived.

Thurgood Marshall, who waited tables to get through law school, and who grew into one of the country's best legal brains, was a feared antagonist to his legal opponents. For his tireless work in effecting positive change, he has been the recipient of a host of honors, most notably the NAACP's Spingarn Medal (1946). "My commitments," he once said, "have always been to justice for all people, regardless of race, creed or color." On January 24, 1993, Thurgood Marshall died, but his efforts remain as a constant reminder of the work ahead.

OSCAR MICHEAUX
1884 -1951

The trailblazer for many of today's Black independent film producers was Oscar Micheaux, the first Black to successfully enter this once all-White arena. As a novelist, publisher, producer, distributor, and "super salesman," the flamboyant Micheaux barnstormed the country producing films and earning his own niche in cinema history. It was a strange fate for a man whose first interest was in farming.

Ocsar Micheaux's rise to production heights began on a farm near Cairo, Illinois, in 1884, where he was born, the fourth son of five children of former slaves. When he was 17, he left home and became a Pullman porter working on westbound trains. Subsequently, in 1904, he purchased a farm in Gregory County, South Dakota, where he was the only Black in the farming community. He was a successful farmer and friendly with his White neighbors. He was described as an introvert with a touch of pride about himself.

After an unhappy love affair that was followed by a more frustrating marriage, Oscar Micheaux wrote his autobiography, *The Conquest: The Story of a Negro Pioneer.* He published it at his own expense, and it probably would have only been read by few had he not launched his own promotional book tour.

Drawing from his talent for salesmanship, he formed his own publishing company and barnstormed the country touting his books in Black communities nationwide.Taking his promotional abilities to another art form, he adapted his novel, *The Homesteader,* into a film, thereby launching his cinema career. With door-to-door sales tactics, he ventured from town to town pitching his script. His sales success was proved by the fact that he persuaded owners of the 700 movie houses tailored to Black audiences to book his film and pay him in advance.

With money, Micheaux returned to Harlem and convinced friends and relatives to support his movies. His goal was to portray a more upscale side of Black life, producing films reflecting the life of the Black bourgeoisie. He billed many of his actors as the "Black Valentino," the "sepia Mae West," the "colored Cagney" or the "Negro Harlow" after famous White actors and actresses.

An imposing figure, Micheaux was six feet tall and possessed a charming, arresting appearance. He would boldly recruit his actors by approaching total strangers and saying, "You should be in my next film." So successful was this technique that Lorenzo Tucker, his "Black Valentino," once remarked that he "was so imposing, he could talk the shirt off your back and get you to offer the tie to go with it."

Working under a tight budget and tighter time limits, the end-products were technically inferior and artistically substandard. Nevertheless, his films were well-received and he sparked interest in the movies. Among the actors who Micheaux discovered was Paul Robeson, who appeared in his *Body and Soul* in 1924. Robeson went on to huge success here and abroad both as an actor and as a concert-rated singer.

After producing 34 films, Micheaux embarked upon the first Black talkie, *The Exile,* which was distributed in 1931. He boldly explored consciousness-raising themes such as *The Betrayal,* produced in 1948. While on a promotional tour in 1951, Oscar Micheaux died in Charlotte, N.C. His widow, actress Alice B. Russell, became a recluse and refused to comment on her late husband's life, work or impact on the film industry. But Micheaux's mark in history was already established.

The Black farmer from South Dakota had not filmed the world in which most Blacks lived. He had pushed aside the stereotypes of Black servants in favor of characters with which audiences could identify.

ISAAC "IKE" MURPHY
1861-1896

There was a time when Blacks were the dominant jockeys in the sport of horse racing. In fact, 14 of the 15 jockeys riding in the first Kentucky Derby were Black. Isaac Murphy galloped onto the pages of sports history as the first Black jockey to win three Kentucky Derbys.

Inducted into the Jockey Hall of Fame in 1956, Issac Murphy is regarded by many as the greatest of all jockeys. In his prime, he probably had the highest winning average of any jockey in racing history.

Isaac Murphy was born Isaac Burns on January 1, 1861, in Lexington, Kentucky - prime horse racing territory. His father, James Burns, was a free man who earned his profession as a bricklayer, but died a prisoner of war, during the Civil War. His mother, was a laundress who worked for Richard Owings of the famed Owings and Williams Racing Stable. It was through this association that Isaac became acquainted with horses and launched his racing career. His mother changed his name to Murphy as a tribute to her father.

At age 14, on September 15, 1875, Isaac brought home his first victory when he rode Glentina at the Crab Orchard Park in Lexington. This would be the first of more than 628 victories in a career that would see him race 1,412 times. By the 1880s, Murphy had amassed such an impressive track record that Lucky Baldwin, a reputed gambler and horse owner, paid Murphy $10,000 to have first call on his services.

In 1884, a set of perverse circumstances proved fortunate for Murphy. He rode a horse named Buchannan in a qualifying race for the Kentucky Derby. The normally composed Murphy was nearly thrown by the horse, which prompted Murphy to argue against riding the horse in the Derby. Despite Murphy's protests, the owners prevailed when they threatened to suspend him if he refused to ride. Reluctantly, Murphy mounted the horse and went on to win his first Kentucky Derby.

Murphy continued to be a dominant force in racing during the decade of the 1880s. He won three runnings of the Hindoo Stakes in 1883, 1885 and 1886. He won the Latonia Derby in Kentucky on May 23, 1887; and he recorded four triumphs in five runnings of the American Derby in Chicago's Washington Park in 1884, 1885, 1886 and 1888. He won a phenomenal 49 of 51 starts at Saratoga, New York, in 1882.

The years 1890 and 1891 proved to be even more spectacular for Murphy. He won two consecutive Kentucky Derbys, in 1890 on Riley, and 1891 on Kingman. But, what has been described as Murphy's sweet moment of revenge occurred on June 25, 1890, at Sheepshead Bay in New York City. Murphy was riding the mount Salvator and he was pitted against his rival, Ed "Snapper" Garrison, a White jockey who rode Tenny. After the starting pistol sounded, the two stayed neck and neck. Garrison was known for pulling ahead in the final stretch, thereby earning what racing fans dubbed "Garrison's Finish." In this race, however, Murphy's consistent ability to match the pace enabled him to ward off any final surges. He was the victor by a head.

After 1891, Murphy's weight problems, plagued him as he ballooned to 140 pounds during the off-season. He dieted strenuously and this continued weight loss eventually sapped his strength, making him vulnerable to infection. In 1895, he caught pneumonia. On February 12, 1896, at the age of 35, Murphy died, leaving a $30,000 estate to his wife, Lucy.

A favorite of fans and sports writers, in his heyday, Murphy won 44 percent of his races. And his record of three Kentucky Derby victories, established in 1884, 1890 and 1891, held until 1948. Having rode some of the greatest mounts, Isaac "Ike" Murphy felt it truly a honor to be classified as one of Americas greatest jockeys.

JAMES "JESSE" OWENS
1913 -1980

There are few athletes whose phenomenal skill have earned them superstar status in the Olympic record books. Jesse Owens, who amazed the world by winning four gold medals in track and field in the 1936 Olympics in Berlin, is one of those. Amid a backdrop of controversy sparked by Adolf Hitler and his theories of White, Aryan Supremacy, Owens' performance demonstrated the absurdity of such theories.

The energy and humility of this superstar captured the hearts of the spectators and the people of Berlin. His triumph was to remain with Owens long after 1936. In later years, as a public speaker, he would explain, "Regardless of his color, a man who becomes a recognized athlete has to learn to walk 10 feet tall. But he must have his dignity off the athletic field, too."

Born James Cleveland Owens on September 12, 1913, in Danville, Alabama, the son of a family of sharecroppers. As a child, he labored in the fields until his family moved to Cleveland, Ohio. While attending the Fairmont Junior High School in Cleveland, he set the world record of 9.4 seconds in the 100-yard dash. In 1930, Owens enrolled at Ohio State University. He had no scholarship, but he did have a job. This income was doubly important because he married his childhood sweetheart, Ruth Solomon, in 1931, when he was 18, and she 16. Three daughters, Gloria, Beverly and Marlene, were born to the couple.

Owens continued his track competitions under the coaching of OSU's Larry Snyder. In 1935, he turned in what critics called the "greatest performance ever seen in a single day in the history of track athletics" when he set a world record in the broad jump, tied his own world record in the 100-yard dash, and set two more world records in the 220-yard dash and the 220-yard low hurdles.

Encouraged, Jesse Owens entered the 1936 World Olympics in Berlin. The atmosphere at the Olympics was tense because Adolph Hitler had proclaimed that Germans were the "master" race. Owens was more than up to the challenge. In the 100-meter dash, he tied the world record at 10.3 seconds; in the 200-meter dash, he shattered the Olympic record in 20.7 seconds; and then, along with his teammates, he won the 400-meter relay. In the broad jump, Owens was pitted against Luz Long of Germany, who was touted by Hitler as the "White Hope." Owens defeated the German in a record-breaking 26 feet, 5 inches. While the German competitor displayed sportsmanlike behavior by congratulating Owens, his leader, Adolph Hitler, refused to make the presentation.

Having earned the title as the greatest track and field athlete of all time, Jessie Owens toured with the Olympic team, following the Olympics, and then returned to Ohio State, where he earned his B.A. degree in 1937. After graduating, he continued to tour and participate in exhibitions until he was 39. However, at the age of 40, he assessed his life and the awesome burden his win had placed on him. He explained, "I was at the point where I hated a track suit. I was getting tired." But his faith in himself and his country never tired. In recognition, he was later awarded the Presidential Medal of Freedom.

In 1944, Owens changed his career direction and moved to Chicago, where he began working with youngsters on the Illinois Youth Commission. He gave unselfishly of his time and talents declaring, "If I .... can help a young person to be a better person today, then I owe it to him to share my experience."

In 1955, Jessie Owens toured India as a goodwill ambassador for the United States. Later, he founded his own public relations firm and nurtured that successful business until poor health forced him into retirement and a move to warmer weather in Tucson, Arizona. After his death, March 30, 1980, Arizona's flags were flown at half-mast, and his body was flown to Chicago for a hero's funeral.

JACKIE ROBINSON
1919 -1972

The date was October 23, 1945. Crowds of reporters were gathered. The two central characters, Branch Rickey, president of the Brooklyn Dodgers, and Jackie Robinson sat down at a table and signed the contract that made history. Robinson was on his way to becoming the first Black to play on a major league baseball team.

Jack Roosevelt Robinson was born in Cairo, Georgia, on January 31, 1919, the son of sharecroppers. His mother moved to Pasadena, California, where Jackie attended public schools. She worked as a maid, and the family was poor. At Muir Technical High School, he exhibited the athletic ability that would later make him a legend. He excelled in four sports; football, baseball, track and basketball. With no money and no scholarships, he had to enter Pasadena Junior College. There he continued to excel in football and baseball.

After two years, Robinson entered the University of California at Los Angeles. He played on the basketball, baseball and football teams and won acclaim in each sport. He was so versatile that one coach called him "the best basketball player in the United States," and a fellow football player called him "probably the greatest ball carrier on the gridiron today."

In 1941, financial problems forced him to leave college, and he played professional football until he was drafted into the Army to serve in World War II. Following the war, Jackie Robinson coached briefly at Sam Houston College in Texas. He then signed on with a professional Black baseball team, the Kansas City Monarchs. During a championship game, Branch Rickey noticed the skill of Jackie Robinson. This set the stage for his historic contract signing in 1945.

In February, 1946, Robinson married Rachel Annetta Isom and that union produced three children. That year, he played on the Dodgers' farm team, the Montreal Royals, with April 18 as the date of his first game as a member of a White professional team. In his second at-bat, he hit a three-run home run. When the game was over, he had made three other hits, scored four times, and stole two bases. By the end of the 1946 season, Robinson had played a critical role in bringing his team to victory in the Little World Series.

In 1947, Robinson moved up to the big time, as first baseman for the Dodgers. At first, Jackie Robinson suffered a host of indignities, including Black cats being thrown on the field and constant harassment. Nevertheless, he maintained his composure and his sense of sportsmanship. He proved by his actions that he merited his history-making role. After only two years, he won the National League's batting championship and its Most Valuable Player Award.

In the process of ending baseball segregation, Rickey and Robinson did much more. Their tours in the South challenged many racial discrimination traditions. Jackie Robinson, with the rest of the team, stayed in hotels where other Blacks were forbidden. He also rode with his White teammates on trains and ate with them in restaurants.

After a decade of playing in the majors, and after seeing other Blacks enter the professional baseball ranks, Robinson retired in 1956 with a lifetime batting average of .311. He received a score of awards during his lifetime. He also authored a number of semi-autobiographical accounts of his life. In retirement, he worked in business, political jobs and for civil rights. He was a vice president of Chock Full O'Nuts and an aide to New York Governor Nelson Rockefeller. In 1962, Robinson was inducted into the Baseball Hall of Fame, the first Black to be so honored.

On October 24, 1972, Jackie Robinson died at the age of 53, in Stamford, Connecticut. As a tribute to his memory, a host of Little League teams are named in his honor. His name is in the history books not only because Rickey decided the time for integration was right, but also because Jackie Robinson was good at his chosen field of endeavor.

JOHN SWEAT ROCK
1825 - 1866

John Sweat Rock faced a formidable enemy, the chief justice of the United States Supreme Court. And only when Chief Justice Roger B. Taney died, could Rock become the first Black ever to be admitted to practice before the U.S. Supreme court. Rock also was one of the first to coin the phrase, "Black is Beautiful."

Historians believe that John Rock was born in 1825, in Salem, New Jersey, to free parents. Rock was educated in the Salem public schools until he was 19. Subsequently, he taught in a one room schoolhouse and gave private lessons from 1844 to 1848. Interested in medicine, Rock began studying under two White physicians, but because he was Black, he was at first denied admission to medical school.

Rock then turned to dentistry and opened an office in Philadelphia in 1850. Later, he earned his M.D. degree from the American Medical College in Philadelphia, moved to Boston, and was admitted to the Massachusetts Medical Society. In 1852, he began practicing both medicine and dentistry.

John Rock was called upon to treat a number of slaves who were being harbored in the area. It was as an outgrowth of this activity that he became an abolitionist. In 1855, he joined the effort to desegregate Boston's public schools. Rock's advocacy activities were delayed when a throat ailment hampered his ability to speak. He decided to go to France for surgery. After the successful operation, the surgeon advised Rock to suspend speaking engagements and to limit his medical practice. Rock heeded the second bit of advice, but continued his abolitionist activities, spearheading a "Black is Beautiful" campaign.

Rock spoke at many major Black meetings. In 1858, he predicted that "sooner or later the clashing of arms will be heard in this country and the Black man's services will be needed." In 1860, he said, "It is not difficult to see that the idea of Black inferiority is a mere subterfuge to bolster up the infamous treatment which greets the colored man in this slavery-cursed land." Two years later, he challenged Boston's discrimination in jobs and public accommodations.

In 1863, when Congress authorized the commissioning of Black troops to fight in the Civil War, Rock turned to recruiting. He was one of the major forces in the formation of the 54th and 55th Massachusetts Infantry Regiments, two segregated units. And, in 1864, as a delegate from Massachusetts to the National Convention of Colored Men in Boston, he pressed for "equal opportunities and equal rights" that "our brave men are fighting for."

His abolitionist activities spurred Rock to earn a law degree. However, Chief Justice Taney, whose rulings frequently supported slavery, prevented Rock from being admitted to practice before the U.S. Supreme Court. When Tanney died in 1864, this obstacle was lifted and Rock was granted the right to his practice. The order that prompted this historic admission noted that "...for the first time a Negro was admitted to practice before that high tribunal: John S. Rock, an attorney of ability and good name in the city of Boston."

Rock was only able to savor his triumph for one year because, in 1885, he caught a cold and later developed tuberculosis. On December 3, 1866, at the age of 41, John Rock died in the home where he lived with his mother and son. He had achieved many goals, but his great contribution was in crusading for Black rights before and during the Civil War. In contrast, Chief Justice Taney, who was an obstacle to Rock's practice before the Supreme Court, died an object of ridicule.

JOHN B. RUSSWURM
1799 - 1851

Two historical "firsts" belong to John Brown Russwurm: one of the first Black college graduates in the United States, and the co-founder of this country's first Black newspaper, Freedom's Journal.

Russwurn was born a slave in Port Antonio, Jamaica, to John Russwurm, a bachelor, and a female slave whose name is not known. In 1807, his father sent him to school in Canada, where schools were better than in Jamaica, and discrimination was less prevalent than in the United States.

In 1812, Russwurm's father left Jamaica and settled in Portland, Maine. There he met and married Susan Blanchard, who raised the boy as her own even after her husband died in 1815. She enrolled him in Hebron Academy, a preparatory school in Maine. Then, in September, 1824, he enrolled in Bowdoin College at Brunswick, Maine, to study for the ministry. Two years later, he became one of the first of his race to graduate from college in this country.

Anxious to be in the center of the free Black population, Russwurm moved to New York City. During the winter of 1826-27, a friend provided a home where he and other Black leaders met and, out of this group, the first Black newspaper in the United States, *Freedom's Journal*, was born on March 16, 1827.

Initially, the *Journal* was co-edited by Russwurm and the Presbyterian minister, Samuel E. Cornish. However, writers from all over the world contributed to it. In its editorial debut, Russwurm set the tone for the Journal's objective by explaining, "We wish to plead our own cause. Too long have others spoken for us." The newspaper's objectives were immediate freedom for slaves, civil and political equality for free Blacks, and the providing of truthful information about Africa.

John Russwurm's courage in this endeavor can be partially measured by his publication of David Walker's *Appeal* in the *Journal*. In this, Walker, a free Boston Black, advocated slave revolts in the South. This caused an uproar in both the North and South. Walker later died of mysterious circumstances.

Within six months, the ministerial duties forced Cornish to resign and Russwurm assumed full control. For the first six months, the *Journal* served its purpose as a platform for the abolitionist struggle. The publication began to examine the problem of colonization and the "national solidarity race movement." Russwurm eventually embraced the belief that Blacks could never enjoy full American citizenship. On February 14, 1829, he announced that he would be resigning to move to Africa to pursue the question of colonization there.

In the African country of Liberia, Russwurm continued to provide a platform for Black causes through the *Liberia Herald* a newspaper he edited. From 1824 to 1836, he was one of the first Black colonial agents for the American Colonization Society. For this, and for other roles, he mastered several African dialects. In 1835, he resigned from the newspaper in protest over efforts of the American Colonization Society to control the publication.

Russwurm refused to let this incident compromise his passion for Africa and, in 1836, he was appointed governor of Maryland, in the Liberia settlement. He proved an efficient and progressive administrator, instituting a variety of reforms including the encouragement of agriculture and trade, the establishment of a court with presiding judges, and the taking of a census in 1843.

On June 9, 1851, death ended John Brown Russwurm's illustrious career. Highly praised for his governing skills, he was survived by his wife, Sara McGill Russwurm, and four of their five children. A monument was erected in his honor and an island was named after him. But his real mark was on the college campus and later as a pioneer in Black journalism.

WILLIAM S. SCARBOROUGH
1852 - 1926

The first noted Black American scholar in the classics was a man born into slavery in the deep South of Georgia. That such a beginning could produce the author of a widely used Greek textbook is a testimony to William Saunders Scarborough, not only a noted Black classical scholar, but also a university president.

William Scarborough was born in Macon, Georgia, in 1852, to Jeremiah, a free man, and Frances Gwynne, a slave of mixed Spanish and Indian heritage. Because his mother was a slave, he was considered one as well. His mother's master, however, was humane and enabled the Scarborough's to live in their own house. William mastered the rudiments of education with the help of a neighboring free family and a White man, J. C. Thomas. By the time he was 6, he read and wrote so proficiently that he could forge passes for the other slaves. At 12, he studied music, and at 15, he graduated from the Lewis High School in Macon.

Scarborough entered Atlanta University and then Oberlin College in Ohio. He graduated from Oberlin in 1875, and returned to teach at Lewis High School in Macon. In 1876, he accepted an appointment as professor of Latin and Greek at Wilberforce University. He later returned to Oberlin Theological Seminary, where he received an M.A. degree in 1878.

In 1881, Scarborough married Sarah C. Bierce of Danby, New York, also on the staff at Wilberforce. That same year, he authored his first scholarly textbook entitled, *First Lessons in Greek*. It displayed his mastery of this language, and he was elected a member of the American Philological Association the following year, the third Black to be so honored. Five years later, he wrote *The Birds of Aristophanes*, a scholarly analysis.

Scarborough became a focus of controversy because his views were opposed to Booker T. Washington's. In a December, 1898, edition of *Forum* entitled, *The Negro Question from the Negro's Point of View*, he criticized why an educated Black man should be given a "pick instead of Greek and Latin, which would open him to the consideration of life's higher aspects." In a more stinging tone in a 1903 article, *The Educated Negro and His Mission*, Scarborough vented his frustration with Black mentality by noting, "We have too many dudes whose ideas do not rise above the possession of a new suit, a cane, a silk hat, patent leather shoes, a cigarette and a good time."

Through articles and lectures, he continued to push his theory that Blacks should gain an enlightened education, while Booker T. Washington advanced the notion that Blacks should master a skill. As Washington's theory gained popularity and as more skill-oriented subjects crept into the curriculum, Scarborough lost his job at Wilberforce in 1892. Later, however, in 1897, he was reinstated and later named vice-president. In 1908, he was named president of Wilberforce, by now financially troubled by debts. However, he was able to receive help from the African Methodist Episcopal church and businessman Andrew Carnegie, which kept the school solvent.

In 1920, Scarborough resigned to go into politics, where he encouraged Blacks to enter the Republican party in Ohio. In 1921, he added another dimension to his career when he was appointed an assistant in farm studies in the Department of Agriculture and, thereby, became an authority on the Black farmer in the South.

After President Warren G. Harding died, his patron, Scarborough retired in December 31, 1924. On September 9, 1926, William Scarborough died in his Ohio home. During an era when some Blacks and most Whites thought all Blacks should wear blue collars, he stood as an example of the scholastic potential of his race.

WILLIAM GRANT STILL
1895 -1978

William Grant Still was America's first Black classical composer; the first Black to write a symphony; the first Black to conduct a radio station orchestra; and in 1936, the first Black to conduct a major American symphony orchestra. Still pioneered so many facets of music that he was known as the "Dean of Afro-American Composers."

William Still was born in Woodville, Mississippi, on May 11, 1895, to a schoolteacher mother and a musician father. His father died when he was an infant and his mother moved to Little Rock, Arkansas. His mother taught literature in a local high school, while William was watched over by his grandmother. Her constant singing of spirituals introduced him early to Black folk music.

Young William began studying the violin. He attended Wilberforce University as a science student, but left to follow his true love, music, by working with various orchestras. It was during this period that he enrolled at the Oberlin Conservatory, where he worked as a waiter and janitor. His teachers became so impressed with his talents that they created a special scholarship to help him.

When World War I erupted in 1914, Still joined the Army and became a violinist in the Army orchestra. Following the war, he worked with W.C. Handy, where he played oboe in the *Shuffle Along* orchestra in 1921. The all-Black band, though popular, was barred from eating and sleeping at many public establishments on their road tours. Still trained at the New England Conservatory and began studying under composer Edgar Varese, an "avant garde" composer whose style influenced Still's later compositions.

During the 1920s, Still successfully tried his hand at composing; and out of this attempt came two serious concert works, *Darker America* (1924) and *From the Land of Dreams* (1925). Meanwhile, Still yearned to create a piece modeled in the Black musical genre. Of this yearning he said, "I wanted to demonstrate how the blues, so often considered a lowly expression, could be elevated to the highest musical level." Out of this desire came Still's composition, *Afro-American Symphony* (1931) which was performed by the Rochester Philharmonic, the first time a symphonic work by a Black composer was performed by a symphony orchestra. Eventually, the work was performed worldwide, as were his two other works, *Africa* and the *Symphony in G Minor.*

During the 1930s, Still composed on a free-lance basis for such musical greats as Artie Shaw and Paul Whiteman. In 1934, he received a Guggenheim fellowship, which allowed him to devote more time to composing music. Out of this came his first opera, *Blue Steel,* which was based on the story of a Black laborer and was patterned from Black folk music.

The remainder of the 1930s saw Still record a number of other firsts. In 1936, he became the first Black to conduct a major American orchestra, when he led the Los Angeles Philharmonic at the Hollywood Bowl, in a program that was totally his own music. And, the New York City Opera Company's presentation of his composition, *Troubled Island,* was the first time a leading opera company had performed the work of a Black composer.

Still married Verna Avery, an operatic writer, and the duo often collaborated on musical compositions. By the 1940s, Still began composing for film and television, including the theme song for Gunsmoke. His triumphs were acknowledged through a host of honorary degrees, awards and scholarships. Through it all, Still never forgot his racial heritage. He broke his most financially rewarding movie contract, when a director insisted on portraying Blacks in a degrading stereotype.

In the 1940s, William Still and his wife moved to California; and it was in Los Angeles on December 3, 1978, that he died. William Grant Still's legacy left more than 100 written works; symphonies, operas, ballets, and spirituals.

DENMARK VESEY
1767 - 1822

In 1822, Denmark Vesey claimed a place in history by organizing the first extensive slave revolt on American soil, in Charleston, South Carolina, in 1822. The plot was simple but daring: Seize the city; kill all who stood in the way; and, if necessary, escape to the Caribbean or Africa.

Denmark Vesey was born in 1767 to unknown parents, possibly in the West Indies. In 1781, Captain Joseph Vesey, a slave agent, captured Denmark and brought him to San Domingo. Vesey's intelligence and appearance impressed the agent, but he sold him anyway. When young Denmark faked a seizure in the sugar fields, he was considered "unsound" and returned to Captain Vesey.

Denmark joined Vesey's stable of slaves first on slave-trading voyages to China and then in Charleston. He proved to be a diligent worker and mastered the carpentry trade. In 1800, when he was 33, Denmark won $1,500 in a lottery and used $600 of it to purchase his freedom. He earned his living as a carpenter and earned the respect of his peers as a lay reader in the newly-established African Methodist Episcopal Church.

Despite having won his freedom, Vesey bemoaned the plight of the slaves still in bondage. He became inspired by reports of Toussaint L'Ouverture's slave revolt in Haiti and pledged to lead a similar insurrection. Using the church as a base, he secretly organized, recruited and mobilized slaves in the Charleston area.

For the next five years, he planned the revolt, until he had organized a 9,000-member army of slaves and freedmen, consisting of those within 100 miles of Charleston as well as a band of slaves from Thomas Island. An arsenal of weapons and vehicles had also been acquired to aid in the revolt.

At first, the date set to begin the insurrection was July 14, 1822, was a night with no moon, a vacation time for Whites, and a Sunday when plantation hands would arouse no suspicion by being in the city. The insurrectionists were to seize all key places such as arsenals and bridges, and eventually make their escape to San Domingo, in the Dominican Republic.

The plot seemed fail-safe because the leaders had exercised extreme secrecy and had avoided interacting with "trusty" slaves who might leak plans to White slave masters. Despite the utmost care, the plot was uncovered by a slave who told his master. The date was moved up to June 16th. Again, the secrecy was betrayed. Seeing the carefully mapped-out-plan ruined, Vesey tried unsuccessfully to get word to other units. But White authorities moved fast, arresting key plotters.

On June 22, Vesey was found at the home of an ex-wife and was arrested. He and others stood trial on June 23, 1822, and were hung July 2nd. Before the trials ended, a total of 35 were hanged; 38 were released for lack of evidence; 15 were acquitted; and 43 were sentenced to deportation. The informers were given their freedom and lifetime support.

Vesey became a symbol of martyrdom in the cause of liberty; for, as the chief judge said at Vesey's trial: "It is difficult to imagine what infatuation could have promoted you to attempt an enterprise so wild and visionary. You were a free man, were comparatively wealthy, and enjoyed every comfort ... You had, therefore, much to risk and little to gain."

Vesey's martyrdom has not faded in the many decades since 1822. History has judged him a brave and visionary Black. Typical is the judgment of historian Sterling Stuckey: "Denmark Vesey did lead a conspiracy (which) must be regarded as one of the most courageous ever to threaten the racist foundation of America ... He stands today, as he stood yesterday, as an awesome projection of the possibilities for militant action on the part of a people who have for centuries been made to bow down in fear."

DR. DANIEL HALE WILLIAMS
1856 - 1931

Open heart surgeries of today can be traced back to a forward thinking Black doctor, Dr. Daniel Hale Williams, who in 1893, performed the very first operation. "Dr. Dan," as he was affectionately known, also founded Chicago's Provident Hospital in 1891, and the first Black nurses' training school.

Williams was born in Pennsylvania in 1856, the fifth child of Daniel Williams, Jr., a barber, and Sarah Price Williams, a housewife. The family moved to Wisconsin, when Daniel was a child. He attended Haire's Classical Academy in Janesville and set his sights on studying medicine. In 1878, he apprenticed under the highly-respected Dr. Henry Palmer, and mastered the basics that gained him entry into Chicago Medical College, and an M.D. in 1883.

Dr. Williams set up his practice in Chicago, where he attracted an interracial clientele. His reputation quickly spread and he earned a series of important positions at various Chicago institutions requiring medical services. During this time, he yearned for an institution where Blacks could be trained in various medical professions. In 1891, his dream was realized with the opening of Provident Hospital, which boasted a biracial staff, as well as a nurses' training school. In its first year, the hospital's 12 beds served 189 patients.

The incident that added to the doctor's fame occurred in 1893. James Cornish was stabbed in the chest in a brawl and was sent to Provident with what appeared to be a fatal wound. With Cornish's life in jeopardy, Dr. Dan pursued the only sensible course, he opened Cornish's chest. There, he discovered a tear in the pericardial sac, which required immediate attention. He sutured the wound, concluded the operation and made history by being the first doctor, Black or White, to successfully perform open heart surgery. That Cornish lived another 20 years was proof of the operation's success.

Because of the intricacy of the operation and because the doctor was Black, critics challenged Williams' surgical technique as being the actual first. However, medical records could not uncover any prior record of such surgery. In 1894, Dr. Williams was called to another challenge when President Grover Cleveland appointed him chief surgeon of the Freedmen's Hospital in Washington, D.C. There, he was charged with reorganizing this institution, then the largest Black Hospital in the country. He revitalized the hospital by attracting a 20-doctor biracial staff and partitioning the hospital into several specialties, including a nursing school.

Continuing in seeking to improve the medical profession, in 1895, Dr. Williams founded an interracial medical society in Washington and, that same year, pioneered the founding of the all-Black National Medical Association. While in Washington, D.C., Dr. Williams met and married Alice Johnson, a schoolteacher. In 1898, the couple returned to Chicago, after Williams became frustrated with internal politics at Freedmen's Hospital. He returned to Provident Hospital and also served on the staff of St. Luke's Hospital, where he headed one of the largest gynecological departments in Chicago. He eventually opened his own practice.

In 1913, Williams scored another first when he became the first Black member of the American College of Surgeons. Despite the accolades and awards that were bestowed upon him, Dr. Dan's personal life was not happy. His wife's untimely death in 1924, and a series of other family tragedies left him drained. Disillusioned, he withdrew into a self-imposed exile and died August 4, 1931, at his home in Idlewild, Michigan.

History, however, has given him a permanent place of honor. Whites as well as Blacks owe a debt of gratitude to this pioneering surgeon, Dr. Daniel Hale Williams.

■■■ GEORGE WASHINGTON WILLIAMS ■■■
1849 -1891

It is hard to imagine one excelling as a soldier, minister, journalist, lawyer, and politician in one lifetime. But, such was the case with George Washington Williams, who not only succeeded in all that is mentioned, but also emerged as Americas first Black historian.

George was born, on October 16, 1849, to Ellen and Thomas Williams, in Bedford Spring, Pennsylvania. His mother came from German lineage and excelled in the arts. She, therefore, made sure that George received a good education in Pennsylvania and later in Massachusetts. George was privately tutored for two years. He then entered a private academy, and later completed four years at the Newton Center, another private school.

At age 14, George assumed his uncle's name and joined the Union Army, serving in the Civil War. He distinguished himself and rose to the rank of sergeant major. While an injury forced his discharge, he re-enlisted until he was mustered out at war's end. Still eager for army duty, he joined the Mexican Army. He later returned to the U.S. Army to fight against the Comanche Indians.

By now, religious convictions told him that killing did not suit a Christian. Williams left the Army in 1868 and was baptized in the Baptist Church. He spent six years training at Newton Theological Seminary. While there, he cultivated an interest in the history of Blacks in America and this culminated in his senior oration on "Early Christianity in Africa."

On June 11, 1874, Williams was ordained at the First Baptist Church and dispatched to Boston's Twelfth Street Baptist Church to pastor one of New England's oldest and most important Black congregations. He quickly discovered that the church was in serious financial straits, so he successfully raised funds by penning and selling an 80-page history on the church and its impact on the community. In so doing, he proved his potential to be a great historian.

Williams moved to Washington, D.C., and began publishing a journal, *The Commoner*. It was devoted to politics, arts and events of the day. However, it was a financial failure. Soon afterward, he moved to Cincinnati, Ohio, to pastor the Union Baptist Church.

Realizing that long-fought-for constitutional freedoms could be lost, Williams entered politics, viewing it as the most effective avenue for maintaining the gains won. Although his victory was by a slim margin, in 1879, he became the first Black elected to the Ohio legislature. In office, he introduced many bills, such as those proposing regulation of police in large cities, and the bill to repeal prohibition of interracial marriages in Ohio. None of his bills passed, and he did not seek reelection in 1881. He then launched his next career, when he entered the Cincinnati Law School and was admitted to the Ohio bar in 1881.

Williams had long held a strong interest in history. And, the nation's celebrated centennial turned his attention to that of Black history. In this pursuit, he conducted extensive research and realized the awesome need for a comprehensive study and recording of the significant history of Black Americans. Responding, in 1883, his two-volume work was published: *History of the Negro Race in America 1619-1880; Negroes as Slaves, as Soldiers and as Citizens together with a Preliminary Consideration of the Unity of the Human Family*. Five years later, in 1888, Williams cemented his reputation as a historian by publishing, *History of the Negro Troops in the War of Rebellion 1861-1865*. These were major publishing events, more ambitious than ever before undertaken by a Black.

Williams became a world traveler, always working on behalf of Blacks. In 1891, he died in Blackpool, England, where he had gone hoping that the sea air would ease his tuberculosis. His death put an end to another of his projects; an exposure of the Belgian colonial policy in the Congo. Even in this endeavor, George Williams' active mind was far ahead of its time.

NOTES

TEST YOURSELF

Now that you have familiarized yourself with our Historic Black Firsts in this seventh series of Empak's 'Black History publications, this section, in three parts: MATCH; TRUE/FALSE; MULTIPLE CHOICE/FILL-IN, is designed to help you remember some key points about each notable Black First. (Answers on page 32)

MATCH

I. *Match the column on the right with the column on the left by placing the appropriate alphabetical letter next to the Historic Black First it represents.*

1. Benjamin Oliver Davis, Sr. _____
2. Thurgood Marshall _____
3. Jack Johnson _____
4. Joshua Johnston _____
5. George Washington Williams _____
6. William Grant Still _____
7. William S. Scarborough _____

A) Railroad Agent
B) Historian
C) Supreme Court Justice
D) Painter
E) Heavyweight Champ
F) Classical Scholar
G) Composer
H) Army General

TRUE/FALSE

II. *The True and False statements below are taken from the biographical information given on each of the Historic Black Firsts.*

1. John Sweat Rock was the first Black to be a Supreme Court Justice. _____
2. Jackie Robinson was the first Black player on a National Football League team. _____
3. Jesse Owens won four gold medals in the 1936 World Olympics. _____
4. Isaac Murphy was the first Black to win two Kentucky Derbys. _____
5. Oscar Micheaux was the first Black independent film producer. _____
6. Shirley Chisholm was the first Black woman to win an academy award. _____
7. John Mercer Langston was the first Black elected to public office. _____

MULTIPLE CHOICE/FILL-IN

III. *Complete the statements below by underlining the correct name, or by filling-in the correct answer which you have read in the biographical sketches.*

1. (John Derham, James Augustine Healy, Jack Johnson) was the first Black Catholic priest and bishop in the United States.
2. Patricia Harris was the first Black to serve as U.S. Secretary in a President's _____
3. (Henry A. Flipper, Ralph Bunche, Denmark Vesey) was the first to successfully negotiate peace between the _____ and _____.
4. John Brown Russwurm was the founder of the first Black newspaper, entitled _____.
5. (Paul Laurence Dunbar, William Grant Still, Joshua Johnston) published an anthology of poems entitled "Oak and Ivy."
6. Dr. Daniel Hale Williams made medical history with surgery on a _____.
7. Alain LeRoy Locke was the first Black to become a _____.

CROSSWORD PUZZLE

ACROSS

2. Noted insurrectionist
5. Kentucky Derby Triple Winner
6. Made famous by Branch Rickey
8. Drew portraits of the gentry
10. Noted editor and publisher
14. "The Children's Bishop"
15. Fiesty legislator in Congress
17. West Point graduate
20. Secretary to President
22. Helped integrate the Army
23. Accomplished medical practitioner

DOWN

1. Black poet laureate
3. First Black Composer of note
4. "Li'l Arthur"
7. Nobel Peace Prize
9. Embarrassed Adolph Hitler
11. First Black Historian of note
12. Enhanced movie industry
13. President of Wilberforce Univ.
16. "Mr. Civil Rights"
18. Open heart surgery
19. Successfully became a lawyer
21. Coined term, "Black is beautiful"

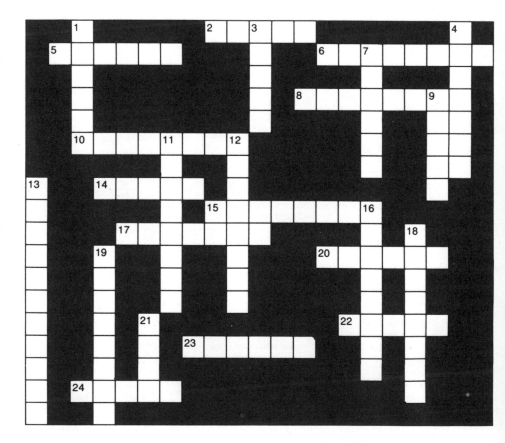

WORDSEARCH

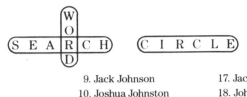

1. Ralph Bunche
2. Shirley Chisholm
3. Benjamin Davis
4. James Derham
5. Paul Dunbar
6. Henry Flipper
7. Patricia Harris
8. Bishop Healy
9. Jack Johnson
10. Joshua Johnston
11. John Langston
12. Alain Locke
13. Thurgood Marshall
14. Oscar Micheaux
15. Isaac Murphy
16. Jesse Owens
17. Jackie Robinson
18. John Rock
19. John Russwurm
20. William Scarborough
21. William Still
22. Denmark Vesey
23. Daniel Williams
24. George Williams

The names of our twenty-four HISTORIC BLACK FIRSTS are contained in the diagram below. Look in the diagram of letters for the names given in the list. Find the names by reading FORWARD, BACKWARDS, UP, DOWN, and DIAGONALLY in a straight line of letters. Each time you find a name in the diagram, circle it in the diagram and cross it off on the list of names. Words often overlap, and letters may be used more than once.

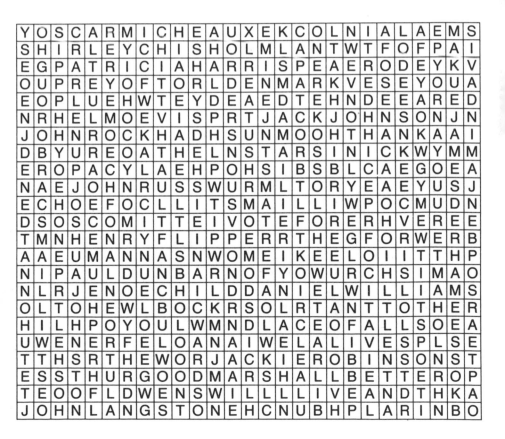

Y	O	S	C	A	R	M	I	C	H	E	A	U	X	E	K	C	O	L	N	I	A	L	A	E	M	S
S	H	I	R	L	E	Y	C	H	I	S	H	O	L	M	L	A	N	T	W	T	F	O	F	P	A	I
E	G	P	A	T	R	I	C	I	A	H	A	R	R	I	S	P	E	A	E	R	O	D	E	Y	K	V
O	U	P	R	E	Y	O	F	T	O	R	L	D	E	N	M	A	R	K	V	E	S	E	Y	O	U	A
E	O	P	L	U	E	H	W	T	E	Y	D	E	A	E	D	T	E	H	N	D	E	E	A	R	E	D
N	R	H	E	L	M	O	E	V	I	S	P	R	T	J	A	C	K	J	O	H	N	S	O	N	J	N
J	O	H	N	R	O	C	K	H	A	D	H	S	U	N	M	O	O	H	T	H	A	N	K	A	A	I
D	B	Y	U	R	E	O	A	T	H	E	L	N	S	T	A	R	S	I	N	I	C	K	W	Y	M	M
E	R	O	P	A	C	Y	L	A	E	H	P	O	H	S	I	B	S	B	L	C	A	E	G	O	E	A
N	A	E	J	O	H	N	R	U	S	S	W	U	R	M	L	T	O	R	Y	E	A	E	Y	U	S	J
E	C	H	O	E	F	O	C	L	L	I	T	S	M	A	I	L	L	I	W	P	O	C	M	U	D	N
D	S	O	S	C	O	M	I	T	T	E	I	V	O	T	E	F	O	R	E	R	H	V	E	R	E	E
T	M	N	H	E	N	R	Y	F	L	I	P	P	E	R	R	T	H	E	G	F	O	R	W	E	R	B
A	A	E	U	M	A	N	N	A	S	N	W	O	M	E	I	K	E	E	L	O	I	I	T	T	H	P
N	I	P	A	U	L	D	U	N	B	A	R	N	O	F	Y	O	W	U	R	C	H	S	I	M	A	O
N	L	R	J	E	N	O	E	C	H	I	L	D	D	A	N	I	E	L	W	I	L	L	I	A	M	S
O	L	T	O	H	E	W	L	B	O	C	K	R	S	O	L	R	T	A	N	T	T	O	T	H	E	R
H	I	L	H	P	O	Y	O	U	L	W	M	N	D	L	A	C	E	O	F	A	L	L	S	O	E	A
U	W	E	N	E	R	F	E	L	O	A	N	A	I	W	E	L	A	L	I	V	E	S	P	L	S	E
T	T	H	S	R	T	H	E	W	O	R	J	A	C	K	I	E	R	O	B	I	N	S	O	N	S	T
E	S	S	T	H	U	R	G	O	O	D	M	A	R	S	H	A	L	L	B	E	T	T	E	R	O	P
T	E	O	O	F	L	D	W	E	N	S	W	I	L	L	L	L	I	V	E	A	N	D	T	H	K	A
J	O	H	N	L	A	N	G	S	T	O	N	E	H	C	N	U	B	H	P	L	A	R	I	N	B	O

MATCH

1.–H	5.–B
2.–C	6.–G
3.–E	7.–F
4.–D	

TRUE/FALSE

1.–FALSE	5.–TRUE
2.–FALSE	6.–FALSE
3.–TRUE	7.–TRUE
4.–FALSE	

MULTIPLE CHOICE/FILL-IN

1.–JAMES AUGUSTINE HEALY
2.–CABINET
3.–RALPH BUNCHE – THE ARABS – ISRAEL
4.–*FREEDOM'S JOURNAL*

5.–PAUL LAURENCE DUNBAR
6.–HEART
7.–RHODES SCHOLAR

CROSSWORD PUZZLE

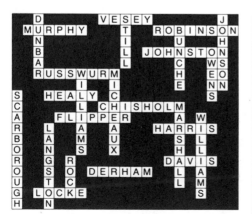

WORD SEARCH

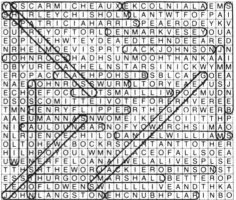

Send to: Empak Publishing Company, 212 E. Ohio St., Suite 300, Chicago, IL 60611—Phone: (312) 642-8364

EPC

Name _____

Affiliation _____

Address _____
P. O. Box numbers not accepted, street address must appear.

City _____ State _____ Zip _____

Phone# (_____) _____ Date _____

Method Of Payment Enclosed: ( ) Check   ( ) Money Order   ( ) Purchase Order

Prices effective 11/1/96 thru 10/31/97

ADVANCED LEVEL

Quantity	ISBN #	Title Description	Unit Price	Total Price
	0-922162-1-8	"A Salute to Historic Black Women"		
	0-922162-2-6	"A Salute to Black Scientists & Inventors"		
	0-922162-3-4	"A Salute to Black Pioneers"		
	0-922162-4-2	"A Salute to Black Civil Rights Leaders"		
	0-922162-5-0	"A Salute to Historic Black Abolitionists"		
	0-922162-6-9	"A Salute to Historic African Kings & Queens"		
	0-922162-7-7	"A Salute to Historic Black Firsts"		
	0-922162-8-5	"A Salute to Historic Blacks in the Arts"		
	0-922162-9-3	"A Salute to Blacks in the Federal Government"		
	0-922162-14-X	"A Salute to Historic Black Educators"		

INTERMEDIATE LEVEL

Quantity	ISBN #	Title Description	Unit Price	Total Price
	0-922162-75-1	"Historic Black Women"		
	0-922162-76-X	"Black Scientists & Inventors"		
	0-922162-77-8	"Historic Black Pioneers"		
	0-922162-78-6	"Black Civil Rights Leaders"		
	0-922162-80-8	"Historic Black Abolitionists"		
	0-922162-81-6	"Historic African Kings & Queens"		
	0-922162-82-4	"Historic Black Firsts"		
	0-922162-83-2	"Historic Blacks in the Arts"		
	0-922162-84-0	"Blacks in the Federal Government"		
	0-922162-85-9	"Historic Black Educators"		

Total Books			❸ Subtotal	
			❹ IL Residents add 8.75% Sales Tax	
	SEE ABOVE CHART ▷		❺ Shipping & Handling	
GRADE LEVEL: 4th, 5th, 6th			❻ Total	

BOOK PRICING ● QUANTITY DISCOUNTS

Advanced Level	Intermediate Level
Reg. $3.49	Reg. $2.29
Order 50 or More	Order 50 or More
Save 40¢ EACH	Save 20¢ EACH
@ $3.09	@ $2.09

❺ SHIPPING AND HANDLING

Order Total	Add
Under $5.00	$1.50
$5.01-$15.00	$3.00
$15.01-$35.00	$4.50
$35.01-$75.00	$7.00
$75.01-$200.00	10%
Over $201.00	6%

In addition to the above charges, U.S. territories, HI & AK, add $2.00. Canada & Mexico, add $5.00. Other outside U.S., add $20.00.

Name _____

Affiliation _____

Street _____
P. O. Box numbers not accepted, street address must appear.

City _____ State _____ Zip _____

Phone (_____) _____ Date _____

Method Of Payment Enclosed:　( ) Check　　　( ) Money Order　　　( ) Purchase Order

Prices effective 11/1/96 thru 10/31/97

PRIMARY LEVEL... KINDERGARTEN, FIRST, SECOND & THIRD GRADE

Quantity	ISBN #	Title Description	Unit Price	Total Price
	0-922162-90-5	"Kumi and Chanti"		
	0-922162-91-3	"George Washington Carver"		
	0-922162-92-1	"Harriet Tubman"		
	0-922162-93-X	"Jean Baptist DuSable"		
	0-922162-94-8	"Matthew Henson"		
	0-922162-95-6	"Bessie Coleman"		
Total Books			❸ Subtotal	
		SEE CHART BELOW ▷	❹ IL Residents add 8.75% Sales Tax	
			❺ Shipping & Handling	
			❻ Total	

KEY STEPS IN ORDERING
❶ Establish quantity needs.　❹ Add tax, if applicable.
❷ Determine book unit price.　❺ Add shipping &handling.
❸ Determine total cost.　❻ Total amount.

BOOK PRICING ● QUANTITY DISCOUNTS
❶ Quantity Ordered	❷ Unit Price
1-49	$3.49
50 +	$3.09

❺ SHIPPING AND HANDLING
Order Total	Add
Under $5	$1.50
$5.01-$15.00	$3.00
$15.01- $35.00	$4.50
$35.01-$75.00	$7.00
$75.01-$200.00	10%
Over $201.00	6%

In addition to the above charges, U.S. territories, HI & AK, add $2.00. Canada and Mexico, add $5.00. Other outside U.S., add $20.00.

Empak Publishing provides attractive counter and floor displays for retailers and organizations interested in the Heritage book series for resale. Please check here ☐ and include this form with your letterhead and we will send you specific information and our special volume discounts.

- The Empak "Heritage Kids" series provides a basic understanding and appreciation of Black history which translates to cultural awareness, self-esteem, and ethnic pride within young African-American children.

- Assisted by dynamic and impressive 4-color illustrations, readers will be able to relate to the two adorable African kids-- Kumi & Chanti, as they are introduced to the inspirational lives and deeds of significant, historic African-Americans.

Black History Materials
Available from Empak Publishing

A Salute To Black History Poster Series
African-American Experience–Period Poster Series
Biographical Poster Series
Heritage Kids Poster Series

Advanced Booklet Series
Instructor's Manuals
Advanced Skills Sheets
Black History Bulletin Board Aids
Instructor's Kits

Intermediate Booklet Series
Teacher's Guides
Intermediate Skill Sheets
Black History Flashcards
Intermediate Reading Certificates
Teacher's Kits

Heritage Kids Booklet Series
Heritage Kids Resource & Activity Guides
Heritage Kids Reading Certificates
Heritage Kids Kits

Black History Videos
Black History Month Activity & Resource Guide
African-American Times–A Chronological Record
African-American Discovery Board Game
African-American Clip Art
Black History Mugs
Black Heritage Marble Engraving
Black History Month Banners (18" x 60")
Say YES to Black History Education Sweatshirts
Say YES to Black History Education T-Shirts

To receive your copy of the Empak Publishing Company's
colorful new catalog, please send $2 to cover postage and handling to:

Empak Publishing Company
Catalog Dept., Suite 300
212 East Ohio Street
Chicago, IL 60611